This journal belongs to

....

You are a beautiful woman of God,
precious to Him in every way. As you seek Him,
He will show you the mysteries of life and unfold
His unique plans for you—a life full of rich blessing.

God cares about you and knows all the desires of
your heart. He is as close as breathing.
Let this journal inspire you to express your
thoughts, record your prayers, embrace your
dreams, and listen to what God is saying to you.

Be strong in the Lord, and may His peace
guide your heart always.

Purity

PROMISE JOURNAL

Ellie Claire
gift & paper expressions

...*inspired by life*

Read the Map

How can a young person live a clean life?
By carefully reading the map of your Word.
I'm single-minded in pursuit of you;
don't let me miss the road signs you've posted.
I've banked your promises in the vault of my heart
so I won't sin myself bankrupt.
Be blessed, GOD;
train me in your ways of wise living.
I'll transfer to my lips
all the counsel that comes from your mouth;
I delight far more in what you tell me about living
than in gathering a pile of riches.
I ponder every morsel of wisdom from you,
I attentively watch how you've done it.
I relish everything you've told me of life,
I won't forget a word of it.

PSALM 119:9–16 THE MESSAGE

I am convinced beyond a shadow of any doubt that the most valuable pursuit we can embark upon is to know God.

KAY ARTHUR

The Secret of Purity

The secret of purity is God. Get a pure heart from God
and you can be supremely happy no matter what the
circumstances and no matter what is going on around you.

BILLY GRAHAM

Strive to soak up the simplicity and purity of Christ.
Try to be more in tune with God and more open to Him,
so that you will be able to see His face.

MOTHER TERESA

As love has its perfect way, it leads us into purity of heart.
When we are perpetually bombarded by the
rapturous experience of divine love, it is only
natural to want to be like the Beloved.

RICHARD J. FOSTER

Life is what we are alive to. It is not length but breadth....
Be alive to...goodness, kindness, purity, love, history,
poetry, music, flowers, stars, God, and eternal hope.

MALTBIE D. BABCOCK

Teach me your ways, O LORD, that I may live according to your truth!
Grant me purity of heart, so that I may honor you.

PSALM 86:11 NLT

Bring Out the Best

So here's what I want you to do, God helping you:
Take your everyday, ordinary life—your sleeping, eating,
going-to-work, and walking-around life—and place
it before God as an offering. Embracing what God
does for you is the best thing you can do for him.
Don't become so well-adjusted to your culture
that you fit into it without even thinking. Instead,
fix your attention on God. You'll be changed from
the inside out. Readily recognize what he wants
from you, and quickly respond to it. Unlike the
culture around you, always dragging you down
to its level of immaturity, God brings the best out
of you, develops well-formed maturity in you.

ROMANS 12:1–2 THE MESSAGE

Anyone who belongs to Christ has become a new person.
The old life is gone; a new life has begun!

2 CORINTHIANS 5:17 NLT

When the world around us staggers from lack of direction,
God offers purpose, hope, and certainty.

GLORIA GAITHER

To Live in Grace

I want first of all...to be at peace with myself.
I want a singleness of eye, a purity of intention,
a central core to my life.... I want, in fact—
to borrow from the language of the saints—
to live "in grace" as much of the time as possible.

ANNE MORROW LINDBERGH

Grace is something you can never get but can
only be given. There's no way to earn it or deserve
it or bring it about anymore than you can deserve
the taste of raspberries and cream or earn
good looks.... A good night's sleep is grace and
so are good dreams. Most tears are grace. The smell
of rain is grace. Somebody loving you is grace.

FREDERICK BUECHNER

Look deep within yourself and recognize what
brings life and grace into your heart. It is this
that can be shared with those around you.
You are loved by God. This is an inspiration to love.

CHRISTOPHER DE VINCK

May God give you more and more grace and peace as you grow in your knowledge of God and Jesus our Lord.

2 PETER 1:2 NLT

Your Sexuality

There's more to sex than mere skin on skin.
Sex is as much spiritual mystery as physical fact.
As written in Scripture, "The two become one."
Since we want to become spiritually one with
the Master, we must not pursue the kind of sex
that avoids commitment and intimacy, leaving us
more lonely than ever—the kind of sex that can
never "become one." There is a sense in which
sexual sins are different from all others. In sexual sin
we violate the sacredness of our own bodies,
these bodies that were made for God-given and
God-modeled love, for "becoming one" with another.
Or didn't you realize that your body is a sacred place,
the place of the Holy Spirit? Don't you see that
you can't live however you please, squandering
what God paid such a high price for? The physical
part of you is not some piece of property belonging
to the spiritual part of you. God owns the whole works.
So let people see God in and through your body.

1 CORINTHIANS 6:16–20 THE MESSAGE

*Physical union with a spouse is a source of friendship, a sharing together
in a great mystery.... It is like a seed from which day by day there grows...
consideration for each other, kindness, tenderness, and confidence.*

PLUTARCH

The Road Ahead

My Lord God, I have no idea where I am going. I do
not see the road ahead of me. I cannot know for
certain where it will end. Nor do I really know myself,
and the fact that I think I am following Your will
does not mean that I am actually doing so.

But I believe that the desire to please You does in fact
please You. And I hope I have that desire in all that I
am doing. I hope that I will never do anything apart from
that desire. And I know that if I do this, You will lead me
by the right road though I may know nothing about it.

Therefore will I trust You always though I may seem
to be lost.... I will not fear, for You are ever with me.
And You will never leave me to face my perils alone.

THOMAS MERTON

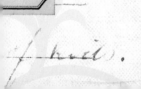

The LORD is my shepherd; I have all that I need....
He guides me along right paths, bringing honor to his name.
Even when I walk through the darkest valley,
I will not be afraid, for you are close beside me.

PSALM 23:1, 3–4 NLT

Better than Gold

The instructions of the LORD are perfect, reviving the soul.
The decrees of the LORD are trustworthy, making wise
the simple. The commandments of the LORD are right,
bringing joy to the heart. The commands of the LORD
are clear, giving insight for living. Reverence for the
LORD is pure, lasting forever. The laws of the LORD are true;
each one is fair. They are more desirable than gold,
even the finest gold. They are sweeter than honey,
even honey dripping from the comb. They are a warning
to your servant, a great reward for those who obey them.

PSALM 19:7–11 NLT

Tune your ears to the world of Wisdom; set your heart
on a life of Understanding. That's right—if you make
Insight your priority, and won't take no for an answer,
searching for it like a prospector panning for gold,
like an adventurer on a treasure hunt, believe me, before you
know it…you'll have come upon the Knowledge of God.

PROVERBS 2:2–5 THE MESSAGE

*It is not the outside riches but the inside ones
that produce happiness.*

DANIEL ORCUTT

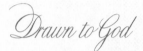

Drawn to God

God longs to give favor—that is, spiritual strength and health—
to those who seek Him, and Him alone. He grants spiritual
favors and victories, not because the one who seeks Him is
holier than anyone else, but in order to make His holy beauty
and His great redeeming power known.... For it is through
the living witness of others that we are drawn to God at all.
It is because of His creatures, and His work in them,
that we come to praise Him.

TERESA OF AVILA

It is only by thinking about great and good things that we
come to love them, and it is only by loving them that we
come to long for them, and it is only by longing for them
that we are impelled to seek after them; and it is only by
seeking after them that they become ours.

HENRY VAN DYKE

It is good for me to draw near to God;
I have put my trust in the LORD GOD.

PSALM 73:28 NKJV

Renew My Spirit

Purify me from my sins, and I will be clean;
wash me, and I will be whiter than snow.

PSALM 51:7 NLT

Create in me a pure heart, O God,
and renew a steadfast spirit within me.
Do not cast me from your presence
or take your Holy Spirit from me.
Restore to me the joy of your salvation
and grant me a willing spirit, to sustain me.

PSALM 51:10–12 NIV

So we're not giving up. How could we! Even though on
the outside it often looks like things are falling apart
on us, on the inside, where God is making new life,
not a day goes by without his unfolding grace.

2 CORINTHIANS 4:16–17 THE MESSAGE

Should we feel at times…discouraged, a simple movement
of heart toward God will renew our powers.
Whatever He may demand of us, He will give us…
the strength and courage that we need.

FRANÇOIS FÉNELON

The Wonder of Living

It's simple things, like a glowing sunset, the sound
of a running stream or the fresh smell in a meadow
that cause us to pause and marvel at the wonder of life,
to contemplate its meaning and significance.
Who can hold an autumn leaf in their hand,
or sift the warm white sand on the beach,
and not wonder at the Creator of it all?

WENDY MOORE

The wonder of living is held within the beauty of silence,
the glory of sunlight…the sweetness of fresh spring air,
the quiet strength of earth, and the love that lies
at the very root of all things.

I marvel at the way
That hope keeps breaking through;
It is the Life in me
That keeps on reenacting
Resurrection.

GLORIA GAITHER

We need to recapture the power of imagination; we shall find
that life can be full of wonder, mystery, beauty, and joy.

SIR HAROLD SPENCER JONES

The heavens are yours, and the earth is yours;
everything in the world is yours—you created it all.

PSALM 89:11 NLT

Out of Sight!

Oh, what joy for those whose disobedience is forgiven,
whose sin is put out of sight! Yes, what joy for
those whose record the LORD has cleared of guilt,
whose lives are lived in complete honesty!
When I refused to confess my sin, my body wasted away,
and I groaned all day long. Day and night your hand
of discipline was heavy on me. My strength evaporated
like water in the summer heat. Finally, I confessed
all my sins to you and stopped trying to hide my guilt.
I said to myself, "I will confess my rebellion to the LORD."
And you forgave me! All my guilt is gone.

PSALM 32:1–5 NLT

For his unfailing love toward those who fear him is as great
as the height of the heavens above the earth. He has removed
our sins as far from us as the east is from the west.

PSALM 103:11–12 NLT

Regardless of your past,
your future is a clean slate.

Pay It Forward

The greatest thing, says someone, a person can do for
his or her heavenly Father is to be kind to some of
His other children. I wonder why it is we are not all
kinder than we are? How much the world needs it. How easily
it is done. How instantaneously it acts. How infallibly
it is remembered. How superabundantly it pays itself back.

HENRY DRUMMOND

A kind heart is a fountain of gladness, making everything
in its vicinity freshen into smiles.

WASHINGTON IRVING

It is in loving—not in being loved—
The heart is blest;
It is in giving—not in seeking gifts—
We find our quest.

An instant of pure love is more precious to God…
than all other good works together, though it may
seem as if nothing were done.

JOHN OF THE CROSS

When you put on a luncheon or a banquet...invite the poor,
the crippled, the lame, and the blind. Then...God will reward
you for inviting those who could not repay you.

LUKE 14:12–14 NLT

Unfailing Love

You are my hiding place;
you protect me from trouble.
You surround me with songs of victory.
The LORD says, "I will guide you along
the best pathway for your life.
I will advise you and watch over you.
Do not be like a senseless horse or mule
that needs a bit and bridle to keep it under control."
Many sorrows come to the wicked,
but unfailing love surrounds those who trust the LORD.
So rejoice in the LORD and be glad,
all you who obey him! Shout for joy,
all you whose hearts are pure!

PSALM 32:7–11 NLT

....

....

....

....

....

....

....

....

....

....

....

....

....

....

A new path lies before us; we're not sure where it leads;
But God goes on before us, providing all our needs.
This path, so new, so different, exciting as we climb,
Will guide us in His perfect will until the end of time.

LINDA MAURICE

Significance of Life

Half the joy of life is in little things taken on the run. Let us run if we must—even the sands do that—but let us keep our hearts young and our eyes open that nothing worth our while shall escape us. And everything is worth its while if we only grasp it and its significance.

All the absurd little meetings, decisions, and skirmishes that go to make up our days. It all adds up to very little, and yet it all adds up to very much. Our days are full of nonsense, and yet not, because it is precisely into the nonsense of our days that God speaks to us words of great significance.

FREDERICK BUECHNER

Every day we live is a priceless gift of God, loaded with possibilities to learn something new, to gain fresh insights.

DALES EVANS ROGERS

Do you not know that in a race all the runners run, but only one gets the prize? Run in such a way as to get the prize.

1 CORINTHIANS 9:24 NIV

That's When You Discover...

You're blessed when you're at the end of your rope.
With less of you there is more of God and his rule.

You're blessed when you feel you've lost what is
most dear to you. Only then can you be embraced
by the One most dear to you.

You're blessed when you're content with just who you are—
no more, no less. That's the moment you find yourselves
proud owners of everything that can't be bought.

You're blessed when you've worked up a good appetite for God.
He's food and drink in the best meal you'll ever eat.

You're blessed when you care. At the moment of
being "care-full," you find yourselves cared for.

You're blessed when you get your inside world—
your mind and heart—put right. Then you can see
God in the outside world.

You're blessed when you can show people how to cooperate
instead of compete or fight. That's when you discover
who you really are, and your place in God's family.

MATTHEW 5:3–9 THE MESSAGE

*God loves us, and the will of love is
always blessing for its loved ones.*

HANNAH WHITALL SMITH

Ask God

God is not really "out there" at all. That restless heart,
questioning who you are and why you were created,
that quiet voice that keeps calling your
name is not just out there, but dwells in you.

DAVID AND BARBARA SORENSEN

There are those who insist that it is a very bad thing
to question God. To them, "why?" is a pride question.
That depends, I believe, on whether it is an
honest search, in faith, for His meaning, or whether
it is the challenge of unbelief and rebellion.

ELISABETH ELLIOT

Come and sit and ask Him whatever is on your heart.
No question is too small, no riddle too simple.
He has all the time in the world.

MAX LUCADO

Keep on asking, and you will receive what you ask for.
Keep on seeking, and you will find. Keep on knocking,
and the door will be opened to you.

MATTHEW 7:7 NLT

A Living, Spirited Dance

Friends. We ask you—urge is more like it—that you
keep on doing what we told you to do to please God,
not in a dogged religious plod, but in a living, spirited
dance. You know the guidelines we laid out for you
from the Master Jesus. God wants you to live a pure life.

Keep yourselves from sexual promiscuity. Learn to appreciate
and give dignity to your body, not abusing it, as is so
common among those who know nothing of God.

Don't run roughshod over the concerns of your brothers
and sisters. Their concerns are God's concerns, and he will take
care of them. We've warned you about this before. God hasn't
invited us into a disorderly, unkempt life but into something
holy and beautiful—as beautiful on the inside as the outside.

1 THESSALONIANS 4:1–7 THE MESSAGE

Each one of us is God's special work of art. Through us,
He teaches and inspires, delights and encourages,
informs and uplifts all those who view our lives.

JONI EARECKSON TADA

Build a Better World

You cannot hope to build a better world without improving the individuals. To that end each of us must work for her own improvement, and at the same time share a general responsibility for all humanity, our particular duty being to aid those to whom we think we can be most useful.

MARIE CURIE

How wonderful it is that nobody need wait a single moment before starting to improve the world.

ANNE FRANK

Every person you meet is an opportunity for kindness.

There's always room for improvement—
it's the biggest room in the house.

LOUISE HEATH LEBER

We become happier, much happier, when we realize that life is an opportunity rather than an obligation.

MARY AUGUSTINE

A good person gives life to others; the wise
person teaches others how to live.

PROVERBS 11:30 NCV

He Made Your Heart

The LORD looks down from heaven and sees the whole
human race. From his throne he observes all
who live on the earth. He made their hearts,
so he understands everything they do....
But the LORD watches over those who fear him,
those who rely on his unfailing love. He rescues
them from death and keeps them alive in times of
famine. We put our hope in the LORD. He is our
help and our shield. In him our hearts rejoice,
for we trust in his holy name. Let your unfailing
love surround us, LORD, for our hope is in you alone.

PSALM 33: 13–15, 18–22 NLT

GOD made my life complete when I placed all the pieces
before him.... Every day I review the ways he works; I try not
to miss a trick. I feel put back together.... GOD rewrote the
text of my life when I opened the book of my heart to his eyes.

PSALM 18:20, 22–24 THE MESSAGE

I know that He who is far outside the whole creation
Takes me within Himself and hides me in His arms.

SYMEON

His Touch

The sunshine dancing on the water, the lulling sound
of waves rolling into the shore, the glittering stars
against the night sky—all God's light, His warmth,
His majesty—our Father of light reaching
out to us, drawing each of us closer to Himself.

WENDY MOORE

Those who draw near to God
One step through doubtings dim,
God will advance a mile
In blazing light to them.

The Lord's chief desire is to reveal Himself to you and,
in order for Him to do that, He gives you abundant grace.
The Lord gives you the experience of enjoying
His presence. He touches you, and His touch is so delightful
that, more than ever, you are drawn inwardly to Him.

MADAME JEANNE GUYON

Draw near to God, and he will draw near to you.

JAMES 4:8 NKJV

Contentment

To be glad of life, because it gives you the chance to
love and to work and to play and to look up at
the stars; to be satisfied with your possessions,
but not contented with yourself until you have made
the best of them;...to think seldom of your enemies,
often of your friends, and every day of Christ;
and to spend as much time as you can, with
body and with spirit in God's out-of-doors—
these are little guideposts on the footpath to peace.

HENRY VAN DYKE

True godliness with contentment is itself great wealth.
After all, we brought nothing with us when we came into
the world, and we can't take anything with us when we leave it.
So if we have enough food and clothing, let us be content.

1 TIMOTHY 6: 6–8 NLT

Do you want to stand out? Then step down. Be a servant.
If you puff yourself up, you'll get the wind knocked
out of you. But if you're content to simply be yourself,
your life will count for plenty.

MATTHEW 23:11–12 THE MESSAGE

Contentment is not the fulfillment of what you want,
but the realization of how much you already have.

No Matter What

It's just a beautiful thing. It's God's grace, because
He knows my heart, and He knows I'm not perfect,
but He still chooses to love me and use me.

JEFF FRANKENSTEIN

The abundant life that Jesus talked about begins
with the unfathomable Good News put simply:
My dear child, I love you anyway.

ALICE CHAPIN

Nothing we can do will make the Father love us less;
nothing we do can make Him love us more.
He loves us unconditionally with an everlasting love.
All He asks of us is that we respond to Him with
the free will that He has given to us.

NANCIE CARMICHAEL

No matter what our past may have held, and no matter how
many future days we have, God stands beside us and loves us.

GARY SMALLEY AND JOHN TRENT

....

....

....

....

....

....

....

....

....

....

....

....

....

....

....

....

I have loved you with an everlasting love;
I have drawn you with loving-kindness.

JEREMIAH 31:3 NIV

He Understands

We do not know what we ought to pray for, but the
Spirit himself intercedes for us with groans that
words cannot express. And he who searches our hearts
knows the mind of the Spirit, because the Spirit
intercedes for the saints in accordance with God's will.

And we know that in all things God works
for the good of those who love him, who have
been called according to his purpose.

ROMANS 8:26–28 NIV

What shall we say about such wonderful things as these?
If God is for us, who can ever be against us?...

And I am convinced that nothing can ever separate
us from God's love. Neither death nor life, neither
angels nor demons, neither our fears for today nor
our worries about tomorrow—not even the powers of
hell can separate us from God's love. No power in the sky
above or in the earth below—indeed, nothing in all creation
will ever be able to separate us from the love of God.

ROMANS 8:31, 38–39 NLT

Pour out your heart to God your Father.
He understands you better than you do.

Live Transparently

The pure in heart live transparently…no guile,
no hidden motives. Rare though the "pure in heart" may be,
this…implies that life can be lived without masks.

CHARLES SWINDOLL

Listen to your life. See it for the fathomless mystery that
it is. In the boredom and pain of it no less than in
the excitement and gladness: touch, taste, smell your
way to the holy and hidden heart of it because in the last
analysis all moments are key moments and life itself is grace.

FREDERICK BUECHNER

"I love you, but I'll love you even more if…" Christ's
love had none of this. No strings, no expectations,
no hidden agendas, no secrets. His love for us was, and is,
up front and clear. "I love you," He says. "Even if you
let Me down. I love you in spite of your failures."

MAX LUCADO

*We throw open our doors to God and discover at the same moment
that he has already thrown open his door to us. We find ourselves...
out in the wide open spaces of God's grace and glory.*

ROMANS 5:2 THE MESSAGE

With All My Heart

Truly God is good to...those whose hearts are pure.
But as for me, I almost lost my footing.
My feet were slipping, and I was almost gone....
Did I keep my heart pure for nothing?
Did I keep myself innocent for no reason?
I get nothing but trouble all day long;
every morning brings me pain....
I was so foolish and ignorant....
Yet I still belong to you;
you hold my right hand.
You guide me with your counsel,
leading me to a glorious destiny.
Whom have I in heaven but you?
I desire you more than anything on earth.
My health may fail, and my spirit may grow weak,
but God remains the strength of my heart;
he is mine forever.

PSALM 73:1–2, 13–14, 22–26 NLT

God is so big He can cover the whole world with His love,
and so small He can curl up inside your heart.

JUNE MASTERS BACHER

The Inner Chamber

Remember, no effort that we make to attain something
beautiful is ever lost. Sometime, somewhere,
somehow, we shall find that which we seek.

HELEN KELLER

Enter into the inner chamber of your mind. Shut out all
things save God and whatever may aid you in seeking God;
and having barred the door of your chamber, seek Him.

ANSELM OF CANTERBURY

If you are seeking after God, you may be sure of this:
God is seeking you much more. He is the Lover,
and you are His beloved. He has promised Himself to you.

JOHN OF THE CROSS

God is not an elusive dream or a phantom to chase, but a
divine person to know. He does not avoid us, but seeks us.
When we seek Him, the contact is instantaneous.

NEVA COYLE

I love those who love me,
and those who seek me find me.

PROVERBS 8:17 NIV

Never Out of Fashion

What you say goes, GOD,
and stays, as permanent as the heavens.
Your truth never goes out of fashion;
it's as up-to-date as the earth when the sun comes up.
Your Word and truth are dependable as ever;
that's what you ordered—you set the earth going.
If your revelation hadn't delighted me so,
I would have given up when the hard times came.
But I'll never forget the advice you gave me;
you saved my life with those wise words.
Save me! I'm all yours.
I look high and low for your words of wisdom....
I see the limits to everything human,
but the horizons can't contain your commands!

PSALM 119:89–94, 96 THE MESSAGE

People change, fashions change, conditions and
circumstances change, but God never changes.
Jesus Christ is the same yesterday, today and forever.

BILLY GRAHAM

Truth is always exciting. Speak it, then.
Life is dull without it.

Pearl S. Buck

Everyday Moments

Much of what is sacred is hidden in the ordinary,
everyday moments of our lives. To see something
of the sacred in those moments takes slowing down
so we can live our lives more reflectively.

KEN GIRE

In the most natural and simple way possible we learn
to pray our experiences by taking up the ordinary
events of everyday life and giving them to God.

RICHARD J. FOSTER

God still draws near to us in the ordinary,
commonplace, everyday experiences and places....
He comes in surprising ways.

HENRY GARIEPY

When we take time to notice the simple things in life,
we never lack for encouragement. We discover
we are surrounded by a limitless hope that's
just wearing everyday clothes.

WENDY MOORE

I know what it is to be in need, and I know what it is to have plenty.
I have learned the secret of being content in any and every situation....
I can do everything through him who gives me strength.

Philippians 4:12–13 NIV

A New Life

So I insist—and God backs me up on this—that there be
no going along with the crowd, the empty-headed,
mindless crowd. They've refused for so long to deal
with God that they've lost touch not only with God but
with reality itself. They can't think straight anymore.
Feeling no pain, they let themselves go in sexual obsession,
addicted to every sort of perversion.

But that's no life for you. You learned Christ! My assumption
is that you have paid careful attention to him, been well
instructed in the truth.... Since, then, we do not have the
excuse of ignorance, everything—and I do mean everything—
connected with that old way of life has to go. It's rotten
through and through.... And then take on an entirely
new way of life—a God-fashioned life, a life renewed
from the inside and working itself into your conduct
as God accurately reproduces his character in you.

EPHESIANS 4:17–24 THE MESSAGE

A study of the nature and character of God is the most practical project anyone can engage in. Knowing about God is crucially important for the living of our lives.

J. I. PACKER

The Pure Essence of God

Although it be good to think upon the kindness of God,
and to love Him and praise Him for it; yet it is far
better to gaze upon the pure essence of Him and to
love Him and praise Him for Himself.

In extravagance of soul we seek His face. In generosity of heart,
we glean His gentle touch. In excessiveness of spirit, we love
Him and His love comes back to us a hundredfold.

TRICIA McCARY RHODES

If a spring is pure and clear, then all the streams that flow
from it must also be clear. This is how the soul becomes
when it understands how to live within God's grace.

TERESA OF AVILA

When the heart is pure it cannot help loving, because
it has discovered the source of love which is God.

JEAN-MARIE BAPTISTE VIANNEY

For the word of the LORD is right and true;
he is faithful in all he does.

Psalm 33:4 NIV

The Child He Embraces

My dear child, don't shrug off God's discipline,
but don't be crushed by it either. It's the child he loves that
he disciplines; the child he embraces, he also corrects.

God is educating you; that's why you must never
drop out. He's treating you as dear children.
This trouble you're in isn't punishment; it's training,
the normal experience of children. Only irresponsible
parents leave children to fend for themselves.
Would you prefer an irresponsible God? We respect
our own parents for training and not spoiling us,
so why not embrace God's training so we can truly live?
While we were children, our parents did what seemed
best to them. But God is doing what is best for us,
training us to live God's holy best. At the time,
discipline isn't much fun. It always feels like it's
going against the grain. Later, of course, it pays off
handsomely, for it's the well-trained who find
themselves mature in their relationship with God.

HEBREWS 12:5–11 THE MESSAGE

Discipline is not an action but an atmosphere.

DAVID JEREMIAH

The Reflective Life

The reflective life is a way of living that prepares
the heart so that something of eternal significance
can be planted there. Who knows what seeds may
come to us, or what harvest will come of them.

KEN GIRE

True prayer is simply a quiet, sincere, genuine conversation
with God. It is a two-way dialogue between friends.

W. PHILLIP KELLER

Genuine heart-hunger, accompanied by sincere seeking
after eternal values, does not go unrewarded.

JUSTINE KNIGHT

When we pray, genuinely pray, the real condition
of our heart is revealed. This is as it should be.
This is when God truly begins to work with us.
The adventure is just beginning.

RICHARD J. FOSTER

I'm asking GOD for one thing, only one thing:
To live with him in his house my whole life long.
I'll contemplate his beauty; I'll study at his feet.

PSALM 27:4 THE MESSAGE

Philosophy Upside-Down

Remember, dear brothers and sisters, that few of you
were wise in the world's eyes or powerful or wealthy
when God called you. Instead, God chose things
the world considers foolish in order to shame those
who think they are wise. And he chose things that are
powerless to shame those who are powerful. God chose
things despised by the world, things counted as
nothing at all, and used them to bring to nothing
what the world considers important. As a result,
no one can ever boast in the presence of God.

1 CORINTHIANS 1:26–29 NLT

If you think you are wise by this world's standards,
you need to become a fool to be truly wise.
For the wisdom of this world is foolishness to God.

1 CORINTHIANS 3:18–19 NLT

He is no fool who gives what he cannot keep
to gain what he cannot lose.

JIM ELLIOT

You Are Valuable

This is the real gift: we have been given the breath of life,
designed with a unique, one-of-a-kind soul that exists forever—
whether we live it as a burden or a joy or with indifference
doesn't change the fact that we've been given the gift of *being*
now and forever. Priceless in value, we are handcrafted
by God, who has a personal design and plan for each of us.

You count on this—the past ended one second ago.
From this point onward, you can be clean, filled with His
Spirit, and used in many different ways for His honor.

CHARLES R. SWINDOLL

You are valuable just because you exist. Not because of
what you do or what you have done, but simply because you are.
Just think about the way Jesus honors you...and smile.

MAX LUCADO

In God's eyes, you are perfectly beautiful and clean.
He sent His own Son to find you and paid an
extravagant price to make you pure and whole.

Look at the birds of the air; they do not sow or reap or store away in barns, and yet your heavenly Father feeds them. Are you not much more valuable than they?

Wisdom Calls Out...

Listen as Wisdom calls out!…
My advice is wholesome.
There is nothing devious or crooked in it.
My words are plain to anyone
with understanding,
clear to those with knowledge.
Choose my instruction rather than silver,
and knowledge rather than pure gold.
For wisdom is far more valuable than rubies.
Nothing you desire can compare with it….
And so, my children, listen to me,
for all who follow my ways are joyful.
Listen to my instruction and be wise.
Don't ignore it.
Joyful are those who listen to me….
For whoever finds me finds life
and receives favor from the LORD.

PROVERBS 8:1, 8–11, 32–35 NLT

Listen to advice and accept instruction,
and in the end you will be wise.

PROVERBS 19:20 NIV

*God's will is determined by His wisdom which always perceives,
and His goodness which always embraces the intrinsically good.*

C. S. Lewis

Radiating Pure Light

It is only when Christ dwells within our hearts,
radiating the pure light of His love through our
humanity that we discover who we are and what
we were intended to be. There is no other
joy that reaches as deep or as wide or as high—
there is no other joy that is more complete.

WENDY MOORE

What greater happiness or higher honor could
we have than to be with God, to be made like
Him and to live in His light?

ANASTASIUS OF SINAI

God specializes in things fresh and firsthand.
His plans for you this year may outshine those
of the past.... He's preparing to fill your days
with reasons to give Him praise.

JONI EARECKSON TADA

Life is a pure flame, and we live by an
invisible sun within us.

SIR THOMAS BROWNE

He will make your innocence radiate like the dawn, and the justice of your cause will shine like the noonday sun.

Psalm 37:6 NLT

Perfect Harmony

Since you have been raised to new life with Christ,
set your sights on the realities of heaven…. So put
to death the sinful, earthly things lurking within you.
Have nothing to do with sexual immorality,
impurity, lust, and evil desires…. Put on your
new nature, and be renewed as you learn to know
your Creator and become like him….

Since God chose you to be the holy people he loves,
you must clothe yourselves with tenderhearted mercy,
kindness, humility, gentleness, and patience. Make
allowance for each other's faults, and forgive anyone
who offends you. Remember, the Lord forgave you,
so you must forgive others. Above all, clothe yourselves
with love, which binds us all together in perfect
harmony. And let the peace that comes from Christ
rule in your hearts. For as members of one body you
are called to live in peace. And always be thankful.

Let the message about Christ, in all its richness,
fill your lives.

Colossians 3:1, 5, 10, 12–16 nlt

Love comes while we rest against our Father's chest.
Joy comes when we catch the rhythms of His heart.
Peace comes when we live in harmony with those rhythms.

KEN GIRE

Share the Love

Friends are an indispensable part of a meaningful life.
They are the ones who share our burdens and multiply
our blessings. A true friend sticks by us in our joys
and sorrows. In good times and bad, we need friends
who will pray for us, listen to us, and lend a comforting
hand and an understanding ear when needed.

BEVERLY LaHaye

Open your hearts to the love God instills....
God loves you tenderly. What He gives you is not
to be kept under lock and key, but to be shared.

MOTHER TERESA

The secret of life is that all we have and are
is a gift of grace to be shared.

LLOYD JOHN OGILVIE

I give you a new command: Love each other. You must love each other as I have loved you. All people will know that you are my followers if you love each other.

JOHN 13:34–35 NCV

A Worthy Life

I...beg you to lead a life worthy of your calling,
for you have been called by God. Always be humble
and gentle. Be patient with each other, making
allowance for each other's faults because of your love.
Make every effort to keep yourselves united in
the Spirit, binding yourselves together with peace.
For there is one body and one Spirit, just as you
have been called to one glorious hope for the future.

EPHESIANS 4:1–4 NLT

Live in peace with each other. And we urge you...
warn those who are idle, encourage the timid, help
the weak, be patient with everyone. Make sure that
nobody pays back wrong for wrong, but always try
to be kind to each other and to everyone else.

1 THESSALONIANS 5:13–15 NIV

No matter what the circumstances are, it is best to pursue behavior that is above reproach, because then you will be respected for your actions.

ROSA PARKS

Consider Your Possibilities

I believe that nothing that happens to me is meaningless,
and that it is good for us all that it should be so,
even if it runs counter to our own wishes. As I see it,
I'm here for some purpose, and I only hope I
may fulfill it. In the light of the great purpose all
our privations and disappointments are trivial.

DIETRICH BONHOEFFER

A span of life is nothing. But the man or woman
who lives that span, they are something. They can
fill that tiny span with meaning, so its quality is
immeasurable, though its quantity may be insignificant.

CHAIM POTOK

What we feel, think, and do this moment influences
both our present and the future in ways we may
never know. Begin. Start right where you are.
Consider your possibilities and find inspiration…
to add more meaning and zest to your life.

ALEXANDRA STODDARD

Leave your simple ways and you will live;
walk in the way of understanding.

PROVERBS 9:6 NIV

You'll Have It All

God is keeping careful watch over us and the future.
The Day is coming when you'll have it all—life healed
and whole. I know how great this makes you feel,
even though you have to put up with every kind of
aggravation in the meantime. Pure gold put in the fire
comes out of it proved pure; genuine faith put through
this suffering comes out proved genuine. When Jesus
wraps this all up, it's your faith, not your gold,
that God will have on display as evidence of his victory.

1 PETER 1:5–7 THE MESSAGE

You have made known to me the path of life;
you will fill me with joy in your presence,
with eternal pleasures at your right hand.

PSALM 16:11 NIV

I would not give one moment of heaven for all the joys and riches of the world, even if it lasted for thousands and thousands of years.

MARTIN LUTHER

Do You Believe?

Do you believe that God is near? He wants you to.
He wants you to know that He is in the midst of your world.
Wherever you are as you read these words, He is present.
In your car. On the plane. In your office, your bedroom,
your den. He's near. And He is more than near. He is active.

MAX LUCADO

Faith is not an effort, a striving, a ceaseless seeking,
as so many earnest souls suppose, but rather a letting go,
an abandonment, an abiding rest in God that nothing,
not even the soul's shortcomings, can disturb.

The world says, "Prove it and I'll believe it."
God says, "Believe it and I'll prove it."

STUART DINNEN

To believe in God starts with a conclusion
about Him, develops into confidence in Him,
and then matures into a conversation with Him.

STUART BRISCOE

*Faith is being sure of what we hope for
and certain of what we do not see.*

HEBREWS 11:1 NIV

A Better Way

LORD, you give light to my lamp.
The LORD brightens the darkness around me....
God is my protection.
He makes my way free from fault.
He makes me like a deer that does not stumble;
he helps me stand on the steep mountains....
You protect me with your saving shield.
You have stooped to make me great.
You give me a better way to live,
so I live as you want me to.

2 SAMUEL 22:29, 33–34, 36–37 NCV

Dear friend, guard Clear Thinking and
Common Sense with your life; don't for a
minute lose sight of them. They'll keep your soul
alive and well, they'll keep you fit and attractive.
You'll travel safely, you'll neither tire
nor trip.... God will be right there with you;
he'll keep you safe and sound.

PROVERBS 3:21–23, 26 THE MESSAGE

*A pure spirit is a sparkling stream, full of clear thought,
and continually renewed in the crystal river of God's love.*

JANET L. WEAVER SMITH

Between You and God

If you are successful, you will win some
false friends and some true enemies;
Succeed anyway.
If you are honest and frank,
people may cheat you;
Be honest and frank anyway....
You see, in the final analysis,
it is between you and God;
it was never between you
and them anyway.

MOTHER TERESA

Accept life daily not as a cup to be drained
but as a chalice to be filled with whatsoever things
are honest, pure, lovely, and of good report.

SIDNEY LOVETT

A good person is not a perfect person;
a good person is an honest person,
faithful and unhesitatingly responsive
to the voice of God in her life. The more
often she responds to that voice,
the easier it is to hear it the next time.

JOHN FISHER

*You prepare a table before me in the presence of my enemies.
You anoint my head with oil; my cup overflows.*

PSALM 23:5 NIV

Sweeter than Honey

How I love your teachings!
I think about them all day long.
Your commands make me wiser than my enemies,
because they are mine forever.
I am wiser than all my teachers,
because I think about your rules....
Your promises are sweet to me,
sweeter than honey in my mouth!
Your orders give me understanding....
Your word is like a lamp for my feet
and a light for my path.
I will do what I have promised
and obey your fair laws....
I will follow your rules forever,
because they make me happy....
You are my hiding place and my shield;
I hope in your word.

PSALM 119:97–99, 103–106, 111, 114 NCV

We may...depend upon God's promises, for...
He will be as good as His word. He is so
kind that He cannot deceive us, so true that
He cannot break His promise.

MATTHEW HENRY

*God makes a promise—faith believes it,
hope anticipates it, patience quietly awaits it.*

Just Being Me

If you believe in God, it is not too difficult to believe
that He is concerned about the universe and all
the events on this earth. But the really staggering
message of the Bible is that this same God cares deeply
about you and your identity and the events of your life.

BRUCE LARSON

I decided for myself that it was okay that I didn't
exactly fit, and I determined that I would become
the person I was meant to be, regardless.

JODY DAVIS

When we live life centered around what others like,
feel, and say, we lose touch with our own identity.
I am an eternal being, created by God. I am an
individual with purpose. It's not what I get from life,
but who I am, that makes the difference.

NEVA COYLE

So be content with who you are, and don't put on airs.
God's strong hand is on you; he'll promote you at the right time.
Live carefree before God; he is most careful with you.

1 PETER 5:6–7 THE MESSAGE

The Call to Action

We are workers together with God, so we beg you:
Do not let the grace that you received from
God be for nothing....

In every way we show we are servants of God: in accepting
many hard things, in troubles, in difficulties,
and in great problems.... We meet those who become
upset with us.... We work hard, and sometimes we
get no sleep or food. We show we are servants of God
by our pure lives, our understanding, patience,
and kindness, by the Holy Spirit, by true love,
by speaking the truth, and by God's power. We use
our right living to defend ourselves against everything.
Some people honor us, but others blame us. Some
people say evil things about us, but others say good things.
Some people say we are liars, but we speak the truth.
We are not known, but we are well known. We seem
to be dying, but we continue to live.... We have much
sadness, but we are always rejoicing. We are poor,
but we are making many people rich in faith.
We have nothing, but really we have everything.

2 CORINTHIANS 6:1, 4–10 NCV

Have you ever thought that in every action of grace in your heart you have the whole omnipotence of God engaged to bless you?

Andrew Murray

The Certainty of Hope

There is not enough darkness in all the world to put
out the light of one small candle.... In moments of
discouragement, defeat, or even despair, there are
always certain things to cling to. Little things usually:
remembered laughter, the face of a sleeping child,
a tree in the wind—in fact, any reminder of something
deeply felt or dearly loved. No one is so poor as not
to have many of these small candles. When they are lighted,
darkness goes away and a touch of wonder remains.

ARTHUR GORDON

You have to have faith that there is a reason you go
through certain things. I can't say I am glad to go
through pain, but in a way one must, in order to
gain courage and really feel joy.

CAROL BURNETT

Because of Christ and our faith in him, we can now come boldly and confidently into God's presence.... I pray that from his glorious, unlimited resources he will empower you with inner strength through his Spirit.

EPHESIANS 3:12, 16 NLT

With Promises Like This...

Don't become partners with those who reject God.
How can you make a partnership out of right and wrong?
That's not partnership; that's war.... Do trust and
mistrust hold hands? Who would think of setting up
pagan idols in God's holy Temple? But that is exactly
what we are, each of us a temple in whom God lives.
God himself put it this way:

"I'll live in them, move into them;
I'll be their God and they'll be my people.
So leave the corruption and compromise;
leave it for good," says God.
"Don't link up with those who will pollute you.
I want you all for myself.
I'll be a Father to you;
you'll be sons and daughters to me."

With promises like this to pull us on, dear friends,
let's make a clean break with everything that defiles or
distracts us, both within and without. Let's make our
entire lives fit and holy temples for the worship of God.

2 Corinthians 6: 14–18; 7:1 the message

God wants His children to establish such a close relationship with Him
that He becomes a natural partner in all the experiences of life.

GLORIA GAITHER

Random Acts of Kindness

Everybody can be great…because anybody can serve.
You don't have to have a college degree to serve…. You only
need a heart full of grace. A soul generated by love.

MARTIN LUTHER KING JR.

Love makes all labor light. We serve with enthusiasm
where we love with sincerity.

HANNAH MORE

When we really love others, we accept them as they are.
We make our love visible through little acts of kindness,
shared activities, words of praise and thanks,
and our willingness to get along with them.

EDWARD E. FORD

All the beautiful sentiments in the world
weigh less than a simple lovely action.

JAMES RUSSELL LOWELL

The royalty among us are those who forget
themselves and serve mankind.

WOODROW WILSON

....

....

....

....

....

....

....

....

....

....

....

....

....

....

....

....

*Love must be sincere.... Be devoted to one another in brotherly love.
Honor one another above yourselves.... Share with God's people
who are in need. Practice hospitality.*

ROMANS 12:9–10, 13 NIV

Say It with Love

When you talk, do not say harmful things,
but say what people need—words that will help
others become stronger. Then what you say
will do good to those who listen to you.
And do not make the Holy Spirit sad.
The Spirit is God's proof that you belong to him.
God gave you the Spirit to show that God will
make you free when the final day comes.

EPHESIANS 4:29–30 NCV

If there's something you need to say to
your loved one, remember to say it lovingly,
as if holding his heart in your hands.

ELLEN SUE STERN

Get rid of all bitterness, rage, anger, harsh words,
and slander, as well as all types of evil behavior.
Instead, be kind to each other, tenderhearted,
forgiving one another, just as God through
Christ has forgiven you.

EPHESIANS 4:31–32 NLT

From the abundance of the heart the mouth speaks.
If your heart is full of love, you will speak of love.

MOTHER TERESA

Life Worth Living

It is the simple things of life that make living worthwhile,
the sweet fundamental things such as love and duty,
work and rest, and living close to nature.

LAURA INGALLS WILDER

Try to make each day reach as nearly as possible the
high water mark of pure, unselfish, useful living.

BOOKER T. WASHINGTON

Let us keep our hearts young and our eyes open that
nothing worth our while shall escape us. And everything
is worth its while if we only grasp it and its significance.

VICTOR CHERBULIEZ

True worth is in *being*, not *seeming*—
In doing, each day that goes by,
Some little good—not in dreaming
Of great things to do by and by.

ALICE CARY

Real joy comes not from ease or riches or from the praise
of people, but from doing something worthwhile.

SIR WILFRED GRENFELL

The wise don't expect to find life worth living;
they make it that way.

God has given each of you a gift from his great variety of spiritual gifts. Use them well to serve one another.

1 PETER 4:10 NLT

Living God's Way

It is obvious what kind of life develops out of trying
to get your own way all the time: repetitive, loveless,
cheap sex; a stinking accumulation of mental and
emotional garbage; frenzied and joyless grabs for happiness;
trinket gods; magic-show religion; paranoid loneliness;
cutthroat competition; all-consuming-yet-never-satisfied
wants; a brutal temper; an impotence to love or
be loved; divided homes and divided lives; small-minded
and lopsided pursuits; the vicious habit of depersonalizing
everyone into a rival; uncontrolled and uncontrollable
addictions…. I could go on…. If you use your
freedom this way, you will not inherit God's kingdom.

But what happens when we live God's way? He brings
gifts into our lives, much the same way that fruit appears
in an orchard—things like affection for others, exuberance
about life, serenity. We develop a willingness to stick
with things, a sense of compassion in the heart,
and a conviction that a basic holiness permeates
things and people. We find ourselves involved in loyal
commitments, not needing to force our way in life,
able to marshal and direct our energies wisely.

GALATIANS 5:19–23 THE MESSAGE

He moves in our lives sharing His very own life with us....
He introduces the exotic fruits of His own person into the
prepared soil of our hearts; there they take root and flourish.

W. PHILLIP KELLER

Sharing Life

Whatever one possesses becomes of double value when
we have the opportunity of sharing it with others.

JEAN-NICOLAS BOUILLY

Love makes burdens lighter, because you divide them.
It makes joys more intense, because you share them.
It makes you stronger, so that you can reach out and
become involved with life in ways you dared not risk alone.

Lord…give me the gift of faith to be renewed and shared
with others each day. Teach me to live this moment only,
looking neither to the past with regret, nor the future with
apprehension. Let love be my aim and my life a prayer.

ROSEANN ALEXANDER-ISHAM

He made you so you could share in His creation,
could love and laugh and know Him.

TED GRIFFEN

If you have any encouragement from being united with Christ, if any comfort from his love...then make my joy complete by being like-minded, having the same love, being one in spirit and purpose.

PHILIPPIANS 2:1–2 NIV

Shine Like the Stars

Do everything without complaining or arguing, so that
you may become blameless and pure, children of God
without fault in a crooked and depraved generation,
in which you shine like stars in the universe as you hold
out the word of life—in order that I may boast on the
day of Christ that I did not run or labor for nothing.

PHILIPPIANS 2:14–16 NIV

Brothers and sisters, think about the things that are good
and worthy of praise. Think about the things that are true and
honorable and right and pure and beautiful and respected....
And the God who gives peace will be with you.

PHILIPPIANS 4:7–9 NCV

If I can think of myself as loved, I can love and accept others.
If I see myself as forgiven, I can be gracious toward others....
If I see myself as full, I can give myself freely to others.

KATHY PEEL

Inconceivable!

Our greatness rests solely on the fact that God in His
incomprehensible goodness has bestowed His love
upon us. God does not love us because we are so valuable;
we are valuable because God loves us.

HELMUT THIELICKE

We are so preciously loved by God that we cannot even
comprehend it. No created being can ever know how
much and how sweetly and tenderly God loves them.

JULIAN OF NORWICH

God has a wonderful plan for each person He has
chosen. He knew even before He created this world
what beauty He would bring forth from our lives.

LOUIS B. WYLY

My life is merely a whisper of the breath of God,
but it *is* His breath, His grace, His life in me.

PHIL JOEL

*Your thoughts—how rare, how beautiful! God, I'll never
comprehend them! I couldn't even begin to count them—
any more than I could count the sand of the sea.*

PSALM 139:17 THE MESSAGE

Happy in Life

Happy people...enjoy the fundamental, often very simple
things of life.... They savor the moment, glad to be alive,
enjoying their work, their families, the good things
around them. They are adaptable; they can bend with
the wind, adjust to the changes in their times,
enjoy the contest of life.... Their eyes are turned
outward; they are aware, compassionate.
They have the capacity to love.

JANE CANFIELD

Happy are those who live pure lives,
who follow the LORD's teachings.
Happy are those who keep his rules,
who try to obey him with their whole heart.
They don't do what is wrong;
they follow his ways.
Lord, you gave your orders
to be obeyed completely.
I wish I were more loyal
in obeying your demands.
Then I would not be ashamed
when I study your commands.
When I learned that your laws are fair,
I praised you with an honest heart.

PSALM 119:1–7 NCV

*As we follow Him who is everlasting we will
touch the things that last forever.*

In Good Company

Savor little glimpses of God's goodness and His majesty,
thankful for the gift of them: winding pathways through
the woods, a bright green canopy overhead, and dappled
sunshine falling all around, warm upon our faces.

WENDY MOORE

The Lord's goodness surrounds us at every moment.
I walk through it almost with difficulty, as through
thick grass and flowers.

R. W. BARBER

God who is goodness and truth is also beauty. It is
this innate human and divine longing, found in the
company of goodness and truth, that is able to recognize
and leap up at beauty and rejoice and know that all is
beautiful, that there is not one speck of beauty under
the sun that does not mirror back the beauty of God.

ROBERTA BONDI

*Let all that I am praise the LORD; may I never
forget the good things he does for me.*

PSALM 103:2 NLT

Personal Trainer

Do not follow foolish stories that disagree with God's truth, but train yourself to serve God. Training your body helps you in some ways, but serving God helps you in every way by bringing you blessings in this life and in the future life, too.... Command and teach these things. Do not let anyone treat you as if you are unimportant because you are young. Instead, be an example to the believers with your words, your actions, your love, your faith, and your pure life.

1 TIMOTHY 4:7–8, 11–12 NCV

Now may God himself, the God of peace, make you pure, belonging only to him. May your whole self— spirit, soul, and body—be kept safe and without fault when our Lord Jesus Christ comes. You can trust the One who calls you to do that for you.

1 THESSALONIANS 5:23–24 NCV

*God did not tell us to follow Him because He needed our help,
but because He knew that loving Him would make us whole.*

IRENAEUS

Why, God?

We may ask, "why does God bring thunderclouds and
disasters when we want green pastures and still waters?"
Bit by bit, we find behind the clouds, the Father's feet;
behind the lightning, an abiding day that has no night;
behind the thunder, a still small voice that comforts
with a comfort that is unspeakable.

There would be no sense in asking why if one did not
believe in anything. The word itself presupposes purpose.
Purpose presupposes a powerful intelligence. Somebody
has to have been responsible. It is because we believe
in God that we address questions to Him.

ELISABETH ELLIOT

At the end of the day, let your mind settle on Him.
Conclude the day as you began it: talking to God.
Thank Him for the good parts.... Question Him about
the hard parts. Seek His mercy. Seek His strength.

MAX LUCADO

We...rejoice in our sufferings, because we know that suffering produces perseverance; perseverance, character; and character, hope. And hope does not disappoint us, because God has poured out his love into our hearts.

ROMANS 5:3–5 NIV

New Life Starting Now

We're being shown how to…take on a God-filled,
God-honoring life. This new life is starting right now,
and is whetting our appetites for the glorious day
when our great God and Savior, Jesus Christ, appears.
He offered himself as a sacrifice to free us from a dark,
rebellious life into this good, pure life, making us
a people he can be proud of, energetic in goodness.

TITUS 2:11–14 THE MESSAGE

Let us draw near to God with a sincere heart in full
assurance of faith, having our hearts sprinkled to cleanse
us from a guilty conscience and having our bodies
washed with pure water. Let us hold unswervingly
to the hope we profess, for he who promised is faithful.
And let us consider how we may spur one another
on toward love and good deeds.

HEBREWS 10:22–25 NIV

*Life begins each morning.... Each morning is the open door
to a new world—new vistas, new aims, new tryings.*

LEIGH MITCHELL HODGES

Adventure Everywhere

Adventure is worthwhile in itself.

AMELIA EARHART

Go forth seeking adventure. Open your eyes, your ears,
your mind, your heart, your spirit, and you'll find adventure
everywhere…. It is in your daily work, whether you are
keeping books, making sales, teaching school, building bridges,
driving a truck…. There is adventure in giving the speech
you are afraid to give. Think of whatever you are doing as
an adventure and watch your life change for the better.

WILFERD A. PETERSON

Security is mostly a superstition. It does not exist in nature.
Life is either a daring adventure or nothing.

HELEN KELLER

There will always be the unknown. There will always be
the unprovable. But faith confronts those frontiers with
a thrilling leap. Then life becomes vibrant with adventure!

ROBERT SCHULLER

Anything, everything, little or big becomes an
adventure when the right person shares it.

KATHLEEN NORRIS

I can't tell you how much I long for you to enter this wide-open, spacious life.... Open up your lives. Live openly and expansively!

2 CORINTHIANS 6:11, 13 THE MESSAGE

Actions vs. Words

But don't just listen to God's word. You must do
what it says. Otherwise, you are only fooling yourselves.
For if you listen to the word and don't obey, it is like
glancing at your face in a mirror. You see yourself,
walk away, and forget what you look like. But if you
look carefully into the perfect law that sets you free,
and if you do what it says and don't forget what
you heard, then God will bless you for doing it.

If you claim to be religious but don't control your tongue,
you are fooling yourself, and your religion is worthless.
Pure and genuine religion in the sight of God the
Father means caring for orphans and widows in
their distress and refusing to let the world corrupt you.

JAMES 1:22–27 NLT

Reach out and care for someone who needs the touch of hospitality.
The time you spend caring today will be a love gift that will blossom
into the fresh joy of God's Spirit in the future.

EMILIE BARNES

God Knows Me

What matters supremely is not the fact that I know God,
but the larger fact which underlies it—the fact that *He knows me*.
I am graven on the palms of His hands. I am never out
of His mind. All my knowledge of Him depends on
His sustained initiative in knowing me. I know Him because
He first knew me, and continues to know me.

J. I. PACKER

Joy comes from knowing God loves me and knows
who I am and where I'm going...that my future
is secure as I rest in Him.

JAMES DOBSON

In those times I can't seem to find God, I rest in
the assurance He knows how to find me.

NEVA COYLE

If you can't pray as you want to, pray as you can.
God knows what you mean.

VANCE HAVNER

God loves me as God loves all people,
without qualification.

ROBERTA BONDI

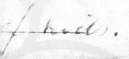

Dear friends, we should love each other, because love comes from God.
Everyone who loves has become God's child and knows God.
Whoever does not love does not know God, because God is love.

1 JOHN 4:7–8 NCV

Lessons for Living

GOD, teach me lessons for living
so I can stay the course.
Give me insight so I can do what you tell me—
my whole life one long, obedient response.
Guide me down the road of your commandments;
I love traveling this freeway!
Give me a bent for your words of wisdom....
Affirm your promises to me—
promises made to all who fear you....
What you say is always so good.
See how hungry I am for your counsel;
preserve my life through your righteous ways!

PSALM 119:33–40 THE MESSAGE

I pray for you constantly, asking God, the glorious
Father of our Lord Jesus Christ, to give you spiritual
wisdom and insight so that you might grow in your
knowledge of God. I pray that your hearts will be
flooded with light so that you can understand the
confident hope he has given to those he called.

EPHESIANS 1:16–18 NLT

*It is God to whom and with whom we travel, and while He is
the End of our journey, He is also at every stopping place.*

ELISABETH ELLIOT

What Can I Do?

Each of us has something different to contribute,
and no matter how small or insignificant it may seem,
it can be for the benefit of all.

LAURITZ MELCHIOR

I am convinced that God has built into all of us an
appreciation of beauty and has even allowed us to
participate in the creation of beautiful things and places.
It may be one way God brings healing to our brokenness,
and a way that we can contribute toward bringing
wholeness to our fallen world.

MARY JANE WORDEN

There is no duty we so much underrate as the duty
of being happy. By being happy we sow anonymous
benefits upon the world.

ROBERT LOUIS STEVENSON

The human contribution is the essential ingredient. It is
only in the giving of ourselves to others that we truly live.

ETHEL PERCY ANDRUS

We have different gifts.... If it is serving, let him serve; if it is teaching, let him teach; if it is encouraging, let him encourage; if it is contributing to the needs of others, let him give generously.

ROMANS 12:6–8 NIV

Extravagant Love

Mostly what God does is love you. Keep company with
him and learn a life of love. Observe how Christ loved us.
His love was not cautious but extravagant. He didn't
love in order to get something from us but to give
everything of himself to us. Love like that.

Don't allow love to turn into lust, setting off a downhill
slide into sexual promiscuity, filthy practices, or bullying
greed. Though some tongues just love the taste of gossip,
those who follow Jesus have better uses for language
than that. Don't talk dirty or silly. That kind of talk
doesn't fit our style. Thanksgiving is our dialect.

EPHESIANS 5:1–4 THE MESSAGE

Love is extravagant in the price it is willing to pay,
the time it is willing to give, the hardships it is willing
to endure, and the strength it is willing to spend. Love never
thinks in terms of "how little," but always in terms of
"how much." Love gives, love knows, and love lasts.

JONI EARECKSON TADA

To love by freely giving is its own reward.
To be possessed by love and to in turn give love
away is to find the secret of abundant life.

GLORIA GAITHER

I Would Be True

How do we become true and good, happy and genuine,
joyful and free?… Only by getting in touch with good,
true, happy, genuine human beings, only by
seeking the company of the strong and the free,
only by catching spontaneity and freedom from those
who are themselves spontaneous and free.

CHARLES MALIK

I would be true, for there are those who trust me;
I would be pure, for there are those who care;
I would be strong, for there is much to suffer;
I would be brave, for there is much to dare.

HOWARD ARNOLD WALTER

If we learn how to give of ourselves, to forgive others,
and to live with thanksgiving, we won't need to seek
happiness. It will seek us.

Let us give all that lies within us…to pure praise,
to pure loving adoration, and to worship from a
grateful heart—a heart that is trained to look up.

AMY CARMICHAEL

Those who refresh others will themselves be refreshed.

PROVERBS 11:25 NLT

Just Do It!

Don't let yourselves get taken in by religious smooth talk.
God gets furious with people who are full of religious
sales talk but want nothing to do with him. Don't even
hang around people like that.

You groped your way through that murk once,
but no longer. You're out in the open now. The bright
light of Christ makes your way plain. So no more
stumbling around.... The good, the right, the true—
these are the actions appropriate for daylight hours.
Figure out what will please Christ, and then do it.

EPHESIANS 5:6–10 THE MESSAGE

The simple fact of being...in the presence of the Lord and
of showing Him all that I think, feel, sense, and experience,
without trying to hide anything, must please Him.

HENRI J. M. NOUWEN

Destiny is not a matter of chance, it is a matter of choice.
It is not a thing to be waited for; it is a thing to be achieved.

WILLIAM JENNINGS BRYAN

Response of the Heart

Love is the response of the heart to the overwhelming goodness
of God, so come in simply and speak to Him in unvarnished
honesty. You may be so awestruck and full of love at
His presence that words do not come. This is all right!

RICHARD J. FOSTER

Fantastic changes can be made in feelings with an honest,
heart-to-heart talk. For in the presence of melted
hearts wrongs are forgiven and hurt hearts healed.

DORIS M. MCDOWELL

Every whispered prayer sent heavenward is our
response to God's embrace.

JANET L. WEAVER SMITH

Gratitude is the homage of the heart, rendered to
God for His goodness.

NATHANIEL PARKER WILLIS

Dear God, whether all my prayers are short or long,
they are a way of keeping me connected to Your love.

LINDA NEUKRUG

My heart has heard you say, "Come and talk with me."
And my heart responds, "LORD, I am coming."

PSALM 27:8 NLT

A Special Purpose

In a wealthy home some utensils are made of gold and silver, and some are made of wood and clay. The expensive utensils are used for special occasions, and the cheap ones are for everyday use. If you keep yourself pure, you will be a special utensil for honorable use. Your life will be clean, and you will be ready for the Master to use you for every good work.

Run from anything that stimulates youthful lusts.
Instead, pursue righteous living, faithfulness,
love, and peace. Enjoy the companionship
of those who call on the Lord with pure hearts.

2 TIMOTHY 2:20–22 NLT

Run for your life from all this. Pursue a righteous life—
a life of wonder, faith, love, steadiness, courtesy.
Run hard and fast in the faith. Seize the eternal life,
the life you were called to.

1 TIMOTHY 6:11 THE MESSAGE

Happiness is living by inner purpose, not by outer pressures.

DAVID AUGSBURGER

I Am My Father's Child

Don't we all long for a father who, even though our mistakes
are written all over the wall, will love us anyway? Don't we
want a father who cares for us in spite of our failures?
We do have that type of a father. A father who is at His
best when we are at our worst. A father whose grace
is strongest when our devotion is weakest.

MAX LUCADO

If God, like a father, denies us what we want now, it is in
order to give us some far better thing later on. The will
of God, we can rest assured, is invariably a better thing.

ELISABETH ELLIOT

God is a rich and bountiful Father, and He does not
forget His children, nor withhold from them anything
which it would be to their advantage to receive.

J. K. MACLEAN

If nothing seems to go my way today, this is my happiness:
God is my Father and I am His child.

BASILEA SCHLINK

Service is the rent we each pay for living. It is not something to do in your spare time; it is the very purpose of life.

MARIAN WRIGHT EDELMAN

What Love Is

Love is not getting, but giving. Not a wild dream of
pleasure and a madness of desire—oh, no—love is not that!
It is goodness and honor and peace and pure living—
yes, love is that and it is the best thing in the world
and the thing that lives the longest.

HENRY VAN DYKE

Love seeks one thing only: the good of the one loved.
It leaves all the other secondary effects to take care of
themselves. Love, therefore, is its own reward.

THOMAS MERTON

Love is not the saying of the words but the giving of the self.

ROBERT LANDER

Joy is love exalted; peace is love in repose; long-suffering
is love enduring; gentleness is love in society; goodness
is love in action; faith is love on the battlefield; meekness
is love in school; and temperance is love in training.

DWIGHT L. MOODY

Go after a life of love as if your life depended on it—
because it does. Give yourselves to the gifts
God gives you. Most of all, try to proclaim his truth.

1 CORINTHIANS 14:1 THE MESSAGE

Wisdom Is...

Are there those among you who are truly wise and
understanding? Then they should show it by living right
and doing good things with a gentleness that comes
from wisdom.... The wisdom that comes from God is
first of all pure, then peaceful, gentle, and easy to please.
This wisdom is always ready to help those who are
troubled and to do good for others. It is always fair
and honest. People who work for peace in a peaceful
way plant a good crop of right-living.

JAMES 3:13, 17–18 NCV

The LORD looks down from heaven on the entire
human race; he looks to see if anyone is truly wise,
if anyone seeks God.

PSALM 14:2 NLT

A wise gardener plants his seeds, then has the good sense not to dig them up every few days to see if a crop is on the way. Likewise, we must be patient as God brings the answers...in His own good time.

QUIN SHERRER

The Big Deal About Sex

Is it a good thing to have sexual relations? Certainly—
but only within a certain context. It's good for a man
to have a wife, and for a woman to have a husband.
Sexual drives are strong, but marriage is strong enough
to contain them and provide for a balanced and fulfilling
sexual life in a world of sexual disorder. The marriage
bed must be a place of mutuality—the husband
seeking to satisfy his wife, the wife seeking to satisfy
her husband. Marriage is not a place to "stand up for
your rights." Marriage is a decision to serve the other,
whether in bed or out.

1 CORINTHIANS 7:1–4 THE MESSAGE

When two persons can share from the very center
of their existence, they experience love in its
truest quality. Marriage is a venture into intimacy,
and intimacy is the opening of one self to another.

JAMES DOBSON

*The only ones among you who will be really happy are those
who have sought and found how to serve.*

ALBERT SCHWEITZER

The Intimacy of God

Our joy will be complete if we remain in His love—
for His love is personal, intimate, real, living,
delicate, faithful love.

MOTHER TERESA

God reads the secrets of the heart. God reads its most intimate
feelings, even those which we are not aware of.

JEAN-NICHOLAS GROU

It's usually through our hard times, the unexpected
and not-according-to-plan times, that we experience
God in more intimate ways. We discover an unquenchable
longing to know Him more. It's a passion that isn't
concerned that life fall within certain predictable lines,
but a passion that pursues God and knows He is
relentless in His pursuit of each one of us.

WENDY MOORE

That is God's call to us—simply to be people who are
content to live close to Him and to renew the kind of
life in which the closeness is felt and experienced.

THOMAS MERTON

....
....
....
....
....
....
....
....
....
....
....
....
....
....
....
....
....
....

*I am the Vine, you are the branches. When you're joined
with me and I with you, the relation intimate and organic,
the harvest is sure to be abundant.*

JOHN 15:5 THE MESSAGE

The Whole Truth

God wants us to grow up, to know the whole truth and
tell it in love—like Christ in everything. We take our lead
from Christ, who is the source of everything we do.
He keeps us in step with each other. His very breath
and blood flow through us, nourishing us so that we
will grow up healthy in God, robust in love.

EPHESIANS 4:14–16 THE MESSAGE

It is an extraordinary and beautiful thing that God,
in creation…works with the beauty of matter;
the reality of things; the discoveries of the senses,
all five of them; so that we, in turn, may hear the grass
growing; see a face springing to life in love and laughter.…
The offerings of creation…our glimpses of truth.

MADELEINE L'ENGLE

Jesus said, "If you hold to my teaching, you are
really my disciples. Then you will know the truth,
and the truth will set you free."

JOHN 8:31–32 NIV

With God our trust can be abandoned, utterly free.
In Him are no limitations, no flaws, no weaknesses.
His judgment is perfect, His knowledge of us is perfect,
His love is perfect. God alone is trustworthy.

EUGENIA PRICE

Ellie Claire Gift & Paper Corp.
Minneapolis 55438
www.ellieclaire.com

Purity
Promise Journal
© 2009 by Ellie Claire Gift & Paper Corp.

ISBN 978-1-935416-49-4

Scripture references are from the following sources: The Holy Bible, New International
Version®, NIV® Copyright © 1973, 1978, 1984 by International Bible Society. Used by permission
of Zondervan. The New King James Version (NKJV). Copyright © 1982 by Thomas Nelson, Inc.
Used by permission. The Holy Bible, New Living Translation (NLT), copyright 1996, 2004.
Used by permission of Tyndale House Publishers, Inc., Wheaton, Illinois. *The Message*.
Copyright © 1993, 1994, 1995, 1996, 2000, 2001, 2002 by Eugene Peterson. Used by
permission of NavPress, Colorado Springs, CO. The New Century Version® (NCV). Copyright
© 1987, 1988, 1991 by Thomas Nelson, Inc. Used by permission. All rights reserved.

Excluding Scripture verses and divine pronouns, in some quotations references to
men and masculine pronouns have been replaced with gender-neutral or
feminine references. Additionally, in some quotations we have carefully updated
verb forms and wordings that may distract modern readers.

Compiled by Barbara Farmer
Cover and Interior design by Lisa and Jeff Franke

Printed in China